# better together*

*This book is best read together, grownup and kid.

 **akidsco.com**

a kids book about

# a kids book about stillbirth

by Emily Gage Alvis

# a kids book about

Text and design copyright © 2024
by A Kids Book About, Inc.

Copyright is good! It ensures that work like this can exist, and more work in the future can be created.

All rights reserved. No part of this publication may be reproduced, distributed, or transmitted in any form or by any means, including photocopying, recording, other electronic or mechanical methods, without the prior written permission of the publisher, except in the case of brief quotations embodied in critical reviews and certain other noncommercial uses permitted by copyright law. For permission requests, write to the publisher.

A Kids Book About, Kids Are Ready, and the colophon 'a' are trademarks of A Kids Book About, Inc.

Printed in the United States of America.

A Kids Book About books are available online: *akidsco.com*

To share your stories, ask questions, or inquire about bulk purchases (schools, libraries, and nonprofits), please use the following email address: *hello@akidsco.com*

Print ISBN: 979-8-89281-044-9
Ebook ISBN: 979-8-89281-045-6

Designed by Rick DeLucco
Edited by Emma Wolf

To my family and friends,

Ryan,

Eloise, Eli, & Owen, August & Miles.

Your love carried me to today.

And my sweet baby Emmett.
I miss you every day.

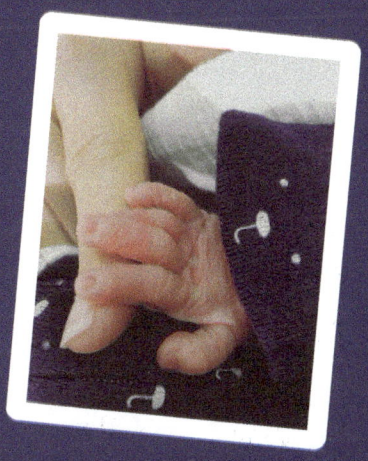

# Intro

Stillborn babies are born into families all around the world. When we honestly talk about this experience, we can broaden our understanding and grieve its occurrence. When we listen and learn from another family's story and get a glimpse of their path toward healing, it can knit the gaps between us. None of us are alone.

I hope my story becomes a bridge to the story you are living into. My words are yours to keep, to offer clarity and healing. In those early days, I wanted so badly to find something honest and comforting to say to my kids when we were trying to put the pieces of this puzzle together. My truth was one that took some time to arrive at. I'm *still* arriving at it.

It's hard when the questions linger, vulnerability floods in, and the truth doesn't feel gentle. I remember thinking so many times: Can I really say this out loud to my kids? Will they still believe there is hope in the world? Will they be OK? Will I be OK? It might be hard to believe, but the answer is yes.

Hi, my name is Emily.

I'm sorry we're meeting this way.

I can only imagine you're reading this book because it's about something you've experienced.

*It's so sad when anyone dies.*

And a baby dying is extremely confusing and sad to all of us—kids and grownups alike.

*I wanted this book so you know you're*

to exist
not alone.

Everything you're thinking and feeling is

# normal.

I don't have to know you personally to believe that is true.

When I was 34 years old,
my son Emmett was stillborn.

*Generally speaking,* when a baby dies before birth or during delivery, they are considered stillborn.

Emmett was the first baby my body tried to make.

*Sadly,* there are many reasons a baby can be stillborn.

Emmett's reason was lack of blood flow from the placenta* to his body.

*The placenta is the organ in the birthing parent's body which nourishes a baby as they grow in the womb.

Our doctors told us he had Down Syndrome* and noticed in his checkups that he wasn't always getting what he needed to grow.

*Down Syndrome is a genetic disorder that causes developmental and physical changes in a person.

We worried about his legs and his heart.

I knew once he arrived, Emmett would have unique needs that required our attention.

And I knew once we had him, we could handle those things.

*But I never anticipated he would die.*

As a society, we have a difficult time comprehending that kids can die—that babies can die.

*It's OK if that's really scary to*

*something to think about.*

It was so hard for me to believe it could happen...but it did.

And I had to find the words to tell others that it happened.

I welcomed 3 kind, beautiful kids into my life when I got married, so I had 3 kids who were waiting for a baby.

Having to look at their sweet faces and tell them Emmett had died was so hard.

*Our cries in those*

*first minutes were a sound I won't forget.*

I know I've never looked that sad in my life, before or after.

I knew my kids were absorbing my feelings about his death and learning how big the experience really was.

And they felt grief—a deep sadness because of this loss—in their own ways.

We encouraged them to do the things that felt normal and exciting at the time: dressing up for Halloween, seeing their friends, or going to a school dance.

*For the most part,* the structure of school felt good, but sometimes, they needed a break.

They also shared their feelings through writing and artwork.

Each kid reacted differently.

When big things happen,
it's natural to have lots of questions.

Why did this happen?

Where are they now?

What do I do now?

These are hard questions—not just for kids, but for grownups, too.

I encourage you to talk about them.

Anything you're wondering about or feeling is normal, and you deserve to be heard in your experiences.

Try not to feel afraid if your grownups don't have all the answers.

*Sometimes,* we just don't know, and sometimes, we need to wait and see.

There's no 1 answer that will make everyone feel OK.

But grieving with people who love you and understand you goes a long way.

We celebrate Emmett's birthday every year.

It's important to remember and be together.

*At his funeral,* we released beautiful paper lanterns.

We still do that with each passing year.

Now we write notes on the lanterns and watch them float away until we can't see them anymore.

We carve pumpkins, we eat takeout, we watch movies—whatever we do, it's special to be together and honor our baby.

It's important to us to connect with Emmett and share our lives with him, to hold space for him in our family.

When someone dies, that person's life and death will always be a part of you.

*What you feel matters and what they meant briefly they were here,*

*a whole lot,
to you, however
matters too.*

Your love and excitement for

*that little baby matters so much.*

# It's OK

to feel really sad.

# It's OK

to be silly or feel angry,
confused, calm, happy,
and anything in between.

# It's OK

to remember.

# It's OK

to forget.

# It's OK

to have good days
and bad ones too.

We feel grief because
there is so much love.

You are loved.
You matter
very much.

And there are so many beautiful things in this world which bring joy, even when things feel hard.

Sometimes, we just need to look a bit closer to find them.

Take it all 1 day at a time, 1 step at a time.

It can, and will, get better.

And I know I just said it,

*but you are
so very loved.*

# Outro

*I* hope you read this book in a comfy spot. I hope you let the tears fall. I hope you held someone close. I hope you talked about your baby. Said their name. Talked about that day. Maybe even mentioned a part you hadn't told anyone before.

Grieving your baby is a forever deal. It won't always feel like that first day, but it will never go away. This process requires vulnerability and bravery you didn't know you had, but I truly believe if you can offer your grief grace and patience, your kids will follow your lead. They will know your love. Your comfort. And understand a bit of your pain. This will validate their own confusion and sadness while also holding them in a safe, assured, and loving place.

So, make art. Cry when you need to. Keep the line of communication open. Pray and worship (if that's right for you). Take walks. Find a forest. Hug your people. Sing. Go to yoga. Go to a support group. Plant things in the ground. And breathe deeply, each and every day.

## About The Author

Emily Gage Alvis (she/her) wrote this book for anyone who loves a baby who was stillborn. It is meant to comfort. It is meant to help. It is meant to shine a gentle light on a silent topic. The words don't come naturally during a time of such immense grief, but Emily hopes her story can help begin a seemingly impossible conversation.

From Emily: *Thank you for reading my story and meeting my Emmett through these words. Seeing his name in print means so much to me and is something I never could have imagined. I wish every mama who endures the death of their baby could write their story, could see their baby's name in meaningful, remembered places, could honor their life in this way. I did not anticipate how healing this process would be for me. I am very thankful.*

*But know there were many days where these words were less hopeful and full of ugly. Know, too, that you are loved, dear reader. And you're not alone. I wish I could hear all of your words about your experiences—I promise, they would make sense to me.*

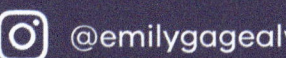

@emilygagealvis

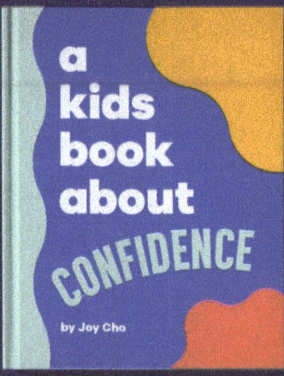
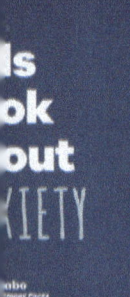

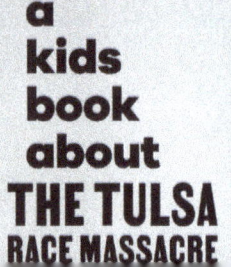

**Discover more at akidsco.com**

www.ingramcontent.com/pod-product-compliance
Lightning Source LLC
Chambersburg PA
CBHW061359010526
44107CB00012B/993